NOT ALL FS ARE BAD

Your Faith & Focus

Ashley M. Martin

WTL Press

To the brave ones out here trusting God and not looking back. Go full steam ahead in the direction of your God-given purpose and destiny.

CONTENTS

INTRODUCTION

Have you ever failed a test?...or a relationship ...or a project ...or felt like you failed at portions of your life?

Have you ever gotten frustrated because you could not finish what you started?

Have you ever found yourself teetering between knowing what you believed for would manifest and questioning whether it would happen or not?

Have you ever just lost your way and needed a nudge to get back on course?

If any of these questions ring a bell, then you're in the right place at the right time, and hopefully you have the right book in your hand.

This book is aimed to equip you with 12 keys that will help you to walk in COMPLETE faith without any doubt and maintain your focus as you partner with God to finish what was started. You may need help getting back on track whether you or someone else messed up.

In today's world, it is not hard to be frustrated, waver, or get distracted. Your faith and focus are in high demand. There are many things competing for them all around - media, social media, the culture, people, environments, habits, and mindsets. These things in and of themselves are not bad but just like anything they can in some way potentially keep your gaze and attention off of the plan and purpose for your life. At times, those very things are essential parts of your lives.

Your loved ones, home, workplace, and health are just a few of the elements of life that make life beautiful and what it is. The challenge for some is often learning how to manage all of these elements and maintain a sense of purpose and follow God's plan for your life.

This reality can be met with the enemy's attempts to frustrate, cast doubt, or throw you off course. It could be sickness, loss of a loved one, a deal that fell through, or an injustice. Unfortunately for the enemy [and fortunately for you], you have a promise from heaven that his shenanigans won't work. Believe and exercise your God-given authority.

I am no stranger to him trying to get a person of course. I have had my share of frustrations, I don't know moments, and distractions I have had to fight and overcome. The good news is that I am also no stranger to God's amazing grace, strength, power, and ability to get you back on track and fully into his plans for your life. #godsplans

With God's help and the Holy Spirit's guidance, this book was written to give you some keys to help you put some things into perspective and equip you to complete your life's work which requires two important things - FAITH and FOCUS.

Do you remember what happened to Peter when he started walking on the water in the book of

Matthew? Matthew 14:22 -33 to be exact. If not, let me refresh your memory. Soon after the miracle of feeding 5,000, Jesus sent his crew (the disciples) ahead of him in a boat and went away to pray for a while by himself. Jesus saw that the wind was growing strong and the waves were starting to get restless. I imagine he was being proactive and thought let me go help my disciples. His caring heart was also a teachable moment for us all.

Jesus arrives on the scene by foot in the middle of the night. Naturally, the disciples freaked out. A person walking on water at 3:00 AM when there are strong winds and restless waves would probably terrify the best of us. Being the Prince of Peace, he calmed them down and said it's me. Peter had some doubts...and some faith.

Peter said if it's really you, tell me to come. I imagine that he had enough faith to know that if it was Jesus and he had given him the empowerment to complete a nature-defying feat that it could happen. Yet he questioned if it was really Jesus, the son of God. Jesus told him, "yes, come."

Packing some courage, Peter gets out of the boat

and starts walking on water.

Go Jesus! Go Peter!

Miracles one after the next, yet mid-walk Peter starts to sink. What happened? He took his eye off of Jesus and looked at the distracting wind and waves around him. When he did that fear came in and he began to sink and cried out for Jesus to save him. Thank God Jesus immediately grabbed him, but he then went on to ask Peter, "why did you doubt me?" He saw and let him know that his faith was little.

In life, there are times when we are met by seemingly impossible circumstances and situations just like Peter and the disciples were in. We encounter strong winds and restless waves in the form of challenges and things that only God can get us out of.

Whether it's a health crisis or an answered prayer you've been waiting on, we must put our faith and focus to use. That's where victory resides. If we're not exercising those, then the other things can take root like fear (the unGodly kind) or forgetting who we are (identity crisis).

As children of the King of Kings, we don't have room nor time to allow the bad Fs like fear, failure, or forgetting who we are to compromise our faith and focus.

While in that boat, the disciples were headed somewhere. Somewhere important. Somewhere with destiny attached to it. They were going to another place where they still had work to do. They were far from finished. There may be some of you reading this who think you're done. Things are over for you, but they are not. You are far from finished.

Maybe you did f—- up something.
Maybe you failed somewhere.
Maybe someone failed you.

You can overcome both sides of the failure coin. Fear and forgetting who you are can be uprooted and God can bring you back into remembrance of who you are and what you're working with as his child. He's also faithful to remind us that if he started a work in us, he will complete it. As you digest these 12 golden keys, remember that not all Fs are bad and you have a few more tools in your box as you walk this thing called life out.

KEY #1 - PRAYER, A DIALOGUE

Never stop praying.

I THESSALONIANS 5:17

Have you gotten lost or lost your child [or another little human being] in the store? One minute the child is walking by your side eyeballing all the things along the shelves. The next minute the child gets distracted and becomes disconnected from you. You see your child fascinated by the objects but are curious as to how he or she will respond when he or she notices you are not around. You stand off to the side as your child calls and searches for you.

"Mama, mama, where are you?"
"Daddy, daddy, where are you?"

Amongst the calling, there is a lot of noise. Carts rushing, customers shopping, scanners beeping, announcements over the loudspeaker, and the store music fill the atmosphere, making it confusing for the child to find you in the midst of it all. Tired from searching, the sobbing child stops. The child has been crying out for you for what seems like forever. He or she feels lost, hopeless, and abandoned. Suddenly, amid tears, you reappear and embrace him or her. The child is delighted to see you and is comforted by your presence. Soon his or her tears dry up. You tell him or her, "Child, I was here all along. You just didn't see or hear me."

There are times in our lives that can seem like we are calling out for God, looking for God, or searching for him for different reasons. It can seem like he is just standing by while you're in need of his presence, his voice, or an answered prayer. He's there and he cares, which is why it is extremely important for us to stay connected to him through prayer.

Just like water is a necessity to the human body, prayer is essential in the life of a believer. A child of God absolutely cannot exist without it. You can exist but I'm not sure what type of existence you'll experience without it. **Prayer is like oxygen, ensuring that your spiritual life is vibrant and healthy.** Between inhales and exhales of life, you need a consistent and constant tool to ensure you are communicating with the one who controls and upholds it all. Prayer is one of the most important ways of staying intimate with God. It allows you to share your heart and it allows God to share his. Yes, he wants to share things with you as well.

This easy yet critical process, communication, is a part of everyday life. Without it, systems would not work, goals would not be met, and relationships would crumble. Likewise, prayer is the glue that holds your relationship with God in tack. I'd even add that it's one of the keys to holding our relationships with human beings intact.

Scripture reveals much about how to pray when to pray, and even for whom to pray (Ephesians 6:8; Matthew 6:9-13; I Timothy 2: 1-2). Many of us have no problem telling God what is on our minds.

"God, I need this. Lord, I want that. Oh Father, please help me with this." Making requests to God can be as easy as giving orders at a restaurant, but it's not. One of the things we often have to be reminded of is that prayer is a dialogue. It's a conversation. The best conversations are not one-sided. It requires that we get quiet and listen for God's voice. To hear what he is saying we have to discipline ourselves - our spirits, minds, and mouths to hear what the Holy Spirit is saying.

Learning to be still and listen for the voice of God can dramatically change your life. It's in the stillness and listening that you gain revelation and realization. Revelation is the act or process of disclosing something previously secret or obscure. Realization is coming to understand something clearly. He discloses precious information to us, giving us strategy, clarity, and direction.

Sometimes our lives and minds are so full of distractions that it can be hard to hear. Just like static on a radio that makes it difficult to hear a song clearly, distractions can make it hard to hear God's voice. You are apt to get lost between what you think you heard and his truth. The more time you spend with God in prayer and other spiritual disciplines, the more you can hear his voice and sense his presence. John 10:27 states "My sheep listen to my voice; I know them, and they follow me."

There may be times in life when it seems as if God does not hear you - your prayers, your pain, your frustrations, or simply your heart. You may think he is just silent. Life gets hectic, demanding, or draining and you wonder, "Lord, are you there? Do you see what I'm going through right now? Do you care?" Like that child, we think he's nowhere to be found. It could be a test but it could also be God waiting on us to turn down all the other voices and volume so that he can get through to us. He's there and he is concerned about you. It is not always easy, but calming and quieting yourself and waiting, puts you in a position to hear or see what you need to from God.

Prayer: *Heavenly Father, help me to communicate better with you. Please clear out distractions in my mind and environment so that I may hear you clearly. I ask that you help me to be still and be a better listener so that I may receive fully all the instructions you have for me. In Jesus Name. Amen.*

Reflect and Act:

1. What is hindering you from having a better prayer life? Is it in your speaking or your listening?

2. Identify common distractions in your communication time with God. It could be people, mindset, environment, or a habit. Create a t-chart in a journal, list your distractions and on the other side write one way you can reduce them.

3. Reflect on a time you prayed and God answered. How did it influence your relationship with him?

KEY #2 - GOD'S PRESENCE

*"You will show me the way of life, granting
me the joy of your presence and the
pleasures of living with you forever."*

PSALMS 16:11

For many years, I retreated with a group of women from all over the country for a few days at a state park. The park, perfectly situated on the top of a mountain with cold, crisp air and, at times, ice or snow would greet us there. During our stay, eagles migrated on the mountain. We looked forward to this unique phenomenon every year, but it's not the eagles that draw us there. We came year after year to bask in the presence of God.

It is so fitting that we referred to our gathering as an experience with God. The experience was centered on ministering to the spiritual and physical needs of the women that attended. Prayer, praise, and worship initiated each session. What followed was an awesome move of God through the ministering of His word whether it was a skit, art, or just good teaching. There were empowerment sessions for spiritual development and healthy living as well as marketplace vending. The highlight of the experience was the foot-washing for each woman in attendance. A time of fellowship and refreshing, these days were filled with unexpected moves of the Holy Spirit.

God's presence allowed us to see miraculous shifts in the lives of the women in attendance. If he wasn't there, it would have just been another women's gathering. Because He was there, his love completely overtook us. One of the keys to God showing up for us in that space included a few things but undoubtedly his presence manifested through worship and praise.

Worship allows God to dwell in our midst. Psalms 22:3 tells us, "Yet you are holy, enthroned on the praises of Israel." God inhabits the praises of his people. When we praise and worship God, we get his attention and he dwells with us. It's in his presence you experience the fullness of joy and pleasure. That is why the time on the mountain was such a joyful time. God was there and he can be with us everywhere. We just have to cultivate a lifestyle that allows his presence to manifest.

To me, God's presence is like spending an incredible week at the beach. [Insert your favorite spot.] Imagine relaxing by the water while sipping your favorite beverage and soaking your skin in the sun (or partially), with the sun feeling incredible on your skin especially after coming out of the water. After you return home from your vacation, it is evident by your newly bronzed skin that you have spent some time basking in the sun.

The same is true when we bask in God's presence. We get a spiritual glow that shouts you have been hanging out with the Father. Some telltale signs are a physical manifestation of feeling lighter, your skin a bit brighter, and overall good energy. The other indicators of some time with God include peace, joy, and love. There may be chaos all around you but when you've been in his presence there is a peace that surpasses all understanding. You may have gone through or be going through the fire but there is no stench of smoke on you. You may have lost everything that externally made you secure but you are confident that God has you and will restore you.

The results of being in God's presence are vital to completing any assignment, fulfilling your divine purpose, and experiencing his fullness in your life.

> *God's presence is not just limited to a mountaintop experience. You have access to him daily. To obtain his presence in your life you must do three things. Be persistent, consistent, and expectant.*

Persistence in pursuing God means you are firm and don't give up chasing after him. Remember worship and praise invites him in. So chase after him through your worship. Pursue him with your praise.

We must be **consistent** in our pursuit after His presence. Pursuing God is not a one time thing. There should be a harmony and steady continuity to worshiping him. Make it a part of your daily routine. Don't allow your location to limit your worship. Worship him in your car, in the shower, or your office. Don't get caught up in worshipping him in one way. Singing, dancing, and being still before him are just a few ways to honor God.

He is guaranteed to show up where you worship. You should **expect** him to show up. Luke 11:9 states, "Ask and it will be given to you; seek and you will find, knock and the door will be opened to you." All you have to do is keep seeking and knocking through your worship. He is ready, waiting to pour out his love, peace, and joy on you. You may end up stumbling upon some blessings as well.

Prayer: *Heavenly Father, thank you for your presence. I need you to lead and guide me. Please help me to be persistent, consistent, and expectant in my pursuit after you. I trust that you meet me in all the ways that I worship. In Jesus' name, Amen.*

Reflect and Act:

1. Find 3 scriptures about praise and worship. Meditate on them. Record any ahas.

2. Practice inviting the presence of God into your

home through worship or playing worship music. What differences do you notice after worshiping him there?

3. Set a few days aside to GO away and seek God. Worship there. Expect to find him. What was your experience like?

KEY #3 - OBEDIENCE

Obedience is better than sacrifice, and submission is better than offering the fat of rams.

1 SAMUEL 15:22, NLT

Many of us are familiar with the scripture that to obey is better than sacrifice. As very human human-beings, this biblical truth is something we need to be reminded of frequently. Our flesh that wants to do its own thing can consistently war against our spirit which (hopefully) wants to please our heavenly father. The impact and outcome of our obedience is influenced by our decisions and choices. Consider Johnnie, who like us at times, needs a little help in this area.

"Johnnie, I am going to the store. This room is a mess! Stop playing that game and start cleaning. Have it clean by the time I get back." Johnnie is in his room entranced in a game of SuperSpeed Chasers. If Johnnie knew what was best for him he would get up immediately and get that room spic and span before his mother returns from the store. Unfortunately, Johnnie decides to continue playing his game of SuperSpeed Chasers. He is so engrossed that he completely forgot the instructions his mother gave him before leaving the store.

Forty-five minutes pass by and Johnnie hears the sound of his mother's car pull up in the driveway. "Oh shoot!" he shouts. As he scrambles to clean up his personal pigsty, he hears his mother's footsteps come closer and closer towards the front door. After she put down her bags on the kitchen counter, she goes to check on Johnnie only to find him scrambling around to clean up his still messy room. You can imagine how happy she was. Because Johnnie did not do as he was told, she took away his video games and he still had to clean his dirty room.

While this story may make you laugh or bring back childhood memories, sometimes we are like this in our relationship with God. We procrastinate or fail to carry through with assignments. God gives us a command to get something together- our health, our finances, our relationships. At times, we drag feet to follow through, and other times we simply don't want to stop playing the games we have been playing. In other cases, we are having so much fun in sin or disobedience, that we simply ignore God's prompting. Besides it impacting us, our obedience or disobedience can impact others.

Obedience looks different for everyone. Some of us may be prompted to stay away from fast food because God is calling us to cleanse our temple. Some of us may be lead to cut out what we feed our eyes and ears. Listening to the latest drama or gossip shouldn't take priority over what God is whispering and telling us. Some of us may be busy spending unnecessary money on things that won't matter to us in a few months while God is urging us to pay off debt and be free from financial bondage. You may have all those areas secure and right standing with God, but could there be another area of your life that God is requiring a different level of obedience out of you?

❖ ❖ ❖

To fulfill your destiny and complete God's call on your life, it's good to do your best to exercise complete and prompt obedience. Complete means whole or comprehensive. Prompt means performed or executed without delay – on time. God is not in the business of giving orders only for us not to be ready to receive and act. If this becomes a part of your pattern, it generally conveys a message that something needs to change. Thank God were his children and he's more than willing to help us do so.

In Johnnie's case, he could not enjoy his fun activity because he was unwilling to put it on hold for 30 minutes. He gives us easy commands like cleaning up your room, but what happens when the obedience God requires of you is not so easy? When it goes against the grain? When it breaks barriers? When it may require something of you you never had to give?

There may be times when God asks you to complete an assignment that you don't understand or seems like a daunting task. You ask God, "You want me to do what?!?" or say things like "God, you want me to love that person. He or she is mean, cold, and just a _____. "(You fill in the blank). We sometimes respond with, "but God, I can't do that or I can't touch that or I can't talk to them" or whatever excuse we try to give God.

When God gives us assignments like these it often leaves you scratching your head. I recall the time I was helping out somewhere. There was one person that clearly could not stand me (or anybody else) it appeared. This person was rude and just very noticeably unhappy. It came across in the person's speech and demeanor. At times this individual was nice, but it was forced and not genuine.

One day while at a meeting, God whispered to me, "Love the hell out of that person." I did a double-take at heaven and asked God for clarity, "What did you say?" Again I heard in that still, small voice, "Love the hell out of that person." I was not feeling this assignment for several reasons. It was clear that the individual did not like me. It was clear that the individual did not like most people. It was clear that their presence made people feel uneasy. In my eyes, I had enough valid evidence that I didn't need to or could not go through with this. It seemed to be just the way this person was. I've learned a while ago that we can't change people, and God is the one that can change hearts and minds. He also gently reminded me that we can influence them.

My questions to God were plenty.

"Ok, Lord, what if this person doesn't let me love her?"

He replied " I'll give her a new heart and put a new spirit in her. I'll remove the heart of stone and replace it with a heart of flesh."

"Ok Lord, how am I supposed to do this?

He replied, " your steps are ordered. Follow my lead."

Now I've had enough experience with God up to this point in my journey to know that although I was not quite feeling this thing and really did not know what to expect, I trusted him that it would work out the way he wanted it to.

He showed me various ways to love this person. It took lots and **lots** and **LOTS** of prayer, fasting, encouragement, more prayer and more encouragement. Ultimately, God's miraculous heart-changing power turned this person around. Moreover, it changed how I saw this individual. I can say after about two years (no, it was not an overnight process) I saw God change this person's countenance from angry to peaceful. I saw God begin to heal this person from the inside out. What was projected onto myself and others had been the accumulation of unresolved issues, hurts, pains, and disappointments. One of the biggest pains this person experienced was hurt by people within the body. There was never any healing from it all.

When that hard ground on this person's heart was finally broken up and God was able to come in and heal and make them whole, they began to find joy in ministering again, being around people again (including me lol), and serving differently. Had I not been obedient to what God told me to do who knows how things would have turned out today. Even when you don't understand, simply obey. You never know what key you hold that could set someone free.

Prayer: *Heavenly Father, help me to obey you completely and promptly. I desire to do your will. Forgive me when I have not been obedient to what you've told me to do. I look forward to a fresh start in obeying you fully and without hesitation. In Jesus' Name. Amen.*

Reflect and Act:

1. List the things that keep you from obeying God. Ask God to help deliver you in those areas.

2. Has there ever been a time when God gave you an assignment you don't want to complete? If so, reflect on what caused you to feel that way.

3. Is God currently calling you to complete an assignment? If so, write down the assignment and at least 3 things you need to complete the assignment. Pray and trust God to supply your needs.

KEY #4 - FAITH & TRUST

Faith is the confidence that what we hope for will actually happen; it gives us assurance about things we cannot see.

HEBREWS 11:1

As a child I remember hearing and singing songs about faith in Sunday school and hearing stories about Joshua, Daniel, and Abraham and the great faith they demonstrated. This faith proved to be one of the keys that led them to great victories.

Faith, believing in what is not yet visible, is

a critical component to successfully complete assignments and walk in your purpose. There is a level of risk that one must assume to see any goal come to fruition. In doing so, you may seem crazy to some or strange to others. You may even question your own moves at times; however, there is a level of hope and trust in God that you must have if you want to do what you're purposed to do. The Bible tells us that without faith, it is impossible to please God (Hebrews 11:6). Imagine that? Your faith pleases the Creator of the universe. Just the contrary, how do you think not exercising your faith makes God feel?

There may be times in life when things hit you and you wonder how am I supposed to have faith through this situation or circumstance. There have been times in my life that it was only my faith in God's word, his promises, and a higher purpose that got me through the day. Have you ever been there? Have you ever been at a point in your life or your journey with God that your faith in a word spoken or the words are written in the Bible was all you had to stand on?

During brunch one Sunday, a friend and I started talking about faith. He mentioned that it's impossible to have faith without trust. In my mind I wondered, "well aren't they the same thing?" That comment made me dig a little deeper into his comment and here's what I discovered.

By definition, trust is the "firm belief in the integrity, ability, and character of a person or thing." It is a "confidence in" or "reliance on" that person or thing. To make sense of it some more, I went to the Bible. Hebrews 11:1 lays it out. "Faith is the substance of things hoped for, the evidence of things not seen." Faith is trusting and believing in what God says and what he shows you in the form or an idea or vision even when you **cannot see physical** evidence of it yet.

Faith is one of the most important aspects of our relationship with God. Besides it pleasing him, trust is necessary for the relationship to work. You'd probably agree that it's a necessity for any relationship to function healthily. In your everyday relationships with spouses, friends, family, framily (friends that are like family), and even colleagues, trust is essential. Trust is even further established and maintained in those moments when you are not with those individuals. When they are away you trust that they will have your best interest in mind.

Trusting when not present works a bit differently with God. Although we cannot physically see him, God is there. The good news is unlike people at times, he will not betray your trust and has your best interest in mind. He will almost always exceed your expectations. I'd argue that he is hands down the best person to be in a relationship with. It's a plus when he sends along others that you can be in a relationship with that bears the same kind of fruit.

Prayer: *Heavenly Father, thank you for the joy and privilege of being in a relationship with you. Forgive me for any time I doubted your goodness. Help me to trust that you are working even when I can't trace you. Help me to stay hopeful and expectant as we both work to see the fruit that faith will produce. In Jesus' name. Amen.*

Reflect and Act:

1. When you hear or see the word faith what else comes to mind? How can this help you at moments when your faith is on the line?

2. Find 3 scriptures that will build up your faith. Memorize and internalize them.

3.Reflect on a time when your faith was tested by something you were working on or working through. What got you to the outcome of what you were believing for? If it wasn't the outcome you were believing for, what helped you to keep going?

KEY #5 - HUMILITY

Therefore, as God's chosen people, holy
and dearly loved, clothe yourselves
with compassion, kindness, humility,
gentleness, and patience.

COLOSSIANS 3:12

I t's pretty amazing to grasp the thought that a part of God stepped down from heaven and came to Earth in the form of a man named Jesus. Jesus who paid a hefty price to save us shows us one of the greatest examples of humility in action. Controversially coming into the world and growing to become a carpenter, Jesus ministered, supernaturally healed, and redeemed people daily during the height of his purpose. Even as a King, he humbled himself and cared for others.

Humility is one of the keys we have that is a requirement to successfully execute an assignment. The grace one needs to ensure that it can happen comes from realizing that you or your efforts are nothing without God's help. Whether it's across a pulpit or in a song, we get messages reminding us to be humble. That must say something about humility's importance.

To fully grasp the part it plays in our lives, it's important to know what it's not so that we can fully understand what it is. Let's debunk some myths about humility and gain the truth about humility.

Myth #1: Humility is the same as low self-esteem.

Truth: Knowing who you are in Christ (Psalm 114:39) and enjoying the fact that a Big and amazing God loves you enough to care to reconcile with you.

Myth #2: Humility means not having confidence.

Truth: Rely on God. Do justly, love mercy and

walk humbly with your God.

Myth #3: Humility means never asking questions.

Truth: Asking when you don't know - "Trust in the Lord with all your heart and lean not unto your own understanding." Proverbs 3:5

Myth #4: Humility means letting people run over you.

Truth: Exercise boundaries. Respects others regardless of a title or position including yourself. " Don't be selfish; don't try to impress others. Be humble, thinking of others as better than yourselves." Philippians 2:3

Myth #5: Humility means you don't know anything.

Truth: True humility means remaining teachable.

There are practical, tangible ways that we can put humility in action. It starts from the inside out with a heart posture that is pure or willing to be purified before God. That means motives, agendas, and thoughts are pleasing in God's sight. If they are not, one of the best ways to purify them is to filter them through God's word. Here are some other ways to make humility a part of your life.

◆ ◆ ◆

Prayer

We discussed prayer in chapter #1, but let's take a deeper dive into some aspects of prayer that can deepen and strengthen our relationship with God, improve our focus, stir up our faith, and allow you to maintain humility. Just as we properly posture our hearts before God, we can posture and position ourselves in prayer. As we seek the face of the one who created it all, here are some ways you can position yourself from the floor to your feet and what they mean.

Laying prostrate before God - stretched out with face on the ground in adoration of or submission to

- Before he was Abraham, Abram fell on his face and talked with God. (Genesis 17:3)

Kneeling - to go down on or rest on one or both

knees

- Before the crucifixion, Jesus knelt before God in the garden of Gethsemane to pray and talk to God. (Luke 22:4)

Standing - upon one's feet

- Jesus encouraged the disciples. He told them that when they stood and pray to forgive anyone who they had something against. (Mark 11:25)

Fasting

Fasting is another way to humble yourself and a way to worship. It's more than just abstaining from food or modifying your meals. Fasting's intent is to transform your heart and mind. Isaiah 58 is the clearest example of the purpose and effect a true fast should have.

"Shout with the voice of a trumpet blast.
Shout aloud! Don't be timid.
Tell my people Israel[a] of their sins!

2

Yet they act so pious!
They come to the Temple every day
and seem delighted to learn all about me.

They act like a righteous nation
that would never abandon the laws of its God.
They ask me to take action on their behalf,
pretending they want to be near me.

3

'We have fasted before you!' they say.
'Why aren't you impressed?
We have been very hard on ourselves,
and you don't even notice it!'
"I will tell you why!" I respond.
"It's because you are fasting to please yourselves.
Even while you fast,
you keep oppressing your workers.
What good is fasting
when you keep on fighting and quarreling?
This kind of fasting
will never get you anywhere with me.
You humble yourselves
by going through the motions of penance,
bowing your heads
like reeds bending in the wind.
You dress in burlap
and cover yourselves with ashes.
Is this what you call fasting?
Do you really think this will please the Lord?

6

"No, this is the kind of fasting I want:
Free those who are wrongly imprisoned;
lighten the burden of those who work for you.
Let the oppressed go free,
and remove the chains that bind people.

7

Share your food with the hungry,
and give shelter to the homeless.
Give clothes to those who need them,
and do not hide from relatives who need your help.

8

"Then your salvation will come like the dawn,
and your wounds will quickly heal.
Your godliness will lead you forward,
and the glory of the Lord will protect you from behind.

9

Then when you call, the Lord will answer.
'Yes, I am here,' he will quickly reply.
"Remove the heavy yoke of oppression.
Stop pointing your finger and spreading vicious rumors!

10

Feed the hungry,
and help those in trouble.
Then your light will shine out from the darkness,
and the darkness around you will be as bright as noon.

11

The Lord will guide you continually,
giving you water when you are dry
and restoring your strength.
You will be like a well-watered garden,
like an ever-flowing spring.

12

Some of you will rebuild the deserted ruins of your cities.
Then you will be known as a rebuilder of walls
and a restorer of homes.

13

"Keep the Sabbath day holy.
Don't pursue your own interests on that day,
but enjoy the Sabbath
and speak of it with delight as the Lord's holy day.
Honor the Sabbath in everything you do on that day,
and don't follow your own desires or talk idly.

14

Then the Lord will be your delight.
I will give you great honor
and satisfy you with the inheritance I promised
to your ancestor Jacob.
I, the Lord, have spoken!"

Service

Helping or assisting others is another way to put humility into action. A genuine act of service from the heart is pleasing to God. Serving others reminds us that life is not all about us. In assisting another, especially on their God-ordained journey, we give glory to God.

Prayer: *Heavenly Father, thank you for the reminders to walk humbly with you and others. Forgive me for the ways I have acted in pride or when I let my ego get in the way of your will. Please continue to allow me to have a humble heart and walk in your ways all the days of my life.*

Reflect and Act:

1. Review the myths and truths about humility. Are they any other myths you would add to the list? Are there any other truths you would add to the list?

2.Reflect on your prayer time. What changes could you make in your posture and positioning?

3.How have your thoughts about fasting changed if at all?

KEY #6 - FILTERING

For the word of God is alive and active.
Sharper than any double-edged sword,
it penetrates even to dividing soul and
spirit, joints and marrow; it judges the
thoughts and attitudes of the heart.

HEBREWS 4:12

"**M**a'am, your water is nasty." This is what the representative of a water filtration company told me after completing an initial analysis of the water in my home at the time. A few months after moving into my house, I was prompted to call someone because I knew something was up with my water. It tasted awful. I noticed changes in my skin and even noticed a difference in my laundry. I knew something had to be done about it.

After completing his analysis, the representative activated the water filtration system that was pre-installed in my house. After activating the system, he poured a glass of water for me. Guess what? I finally had clean water.

We live in a dirty world, full of impurities. Our air is contaminated. Our water is contaminated. If you pause and think about it, most things in our environment require filtering for us to enjoy it. In the same way, we must filter out the impurities that can contaminate our spirits, hearts, and minds.

Life impurities are all those little things that eat at your spirit, heart, and mind- negative thoughts, people's criticism, and even self- criticism. The enemy will use whatever he can try to get you off course. You can cancel his attempts by filtering these contaminants with God's word.

Think of your spirit, heart, and mind as a radio. Frequencies are different and channels vary on a radio. The goal is to be on the frequency of heaven and to have God's channel playing without static or interruptions. It's good to be in tune and hear what's on God's heart. Sometimes, there are little disruptions and interruptions in your channel and other tunes start to come in. You may wonder where did this come from? When those disruptions and interruptions try to come in, you can intercept them with God's word. The enemy may try to send you negative interruptions like these:

"You're Worthless."

"Your Plan Won't Work."

"You Can't Do That."

Intercept his lies with God's truths.

"You're Fearfully and Wonderfully Made." (Psalm

139:14)

" God has Plans to Prosper You." (Jeremiah 29:11)

"You can do All Tings Through Christ that Strengthens You." (Phil 3:14)

Make sure you keep God's truths nearby. Anytime you get distracted by a lie, intercept it. Hearing the word will ensure that the lies of the enemy and anyone else opposing your assignment is minimized.

Prayer: *Heavenly Father, thank you for your word that*

is a filter to life's impurities and the enemy's lies. Please help me to stay in your word so that I have the tools to combat any contaminants. Thank you for refreshing my mind, heart, and spirit with your word. In Jesus' name. Amen

Reflect and Act:

1. Oftentimes the lies that the enemy uses against us are the same. Begin to pay close attention to what he throws your way. Identify at least two scriptures that you can use to combat those lies.

2. Make a list of 5 scriptures that help keep your spirit, heart, and mind pure. Place them strategically to frequently help yourself.

3.What are some other ways that you can filter negativity?

KEY #7 - WISE COUNSEL

*Without wise leadership, a nation falls;
there is safety in having many advisors.*

PROVERBS 11:14

In Meditation XVII, John Donne tells us, "no man is an island, entire of itself; every man is a piece of the continent, a part of the main." We were not meant to do life alone. God never intended for us to be isolated from others. There may be moments that you may be alone but it is never his intent for us to live a life void of other human beings. Even in the beginning, he knew Adam needed

Eve. He knew Joshua needed Caleb. He knew Jesus needed disciples.

God will always have a select group, a remnant, just for you. I like to think of them as the Top 5. This small, intimate group is one that you should go to for prayer, counsel, and at times venting. If you don't have this group established in your life, I highly recommend you seek God and ask him to identify who these people are or to bring them into your life. They are not just anyone and are essential to you completing your purpose. There are a few things that tend to characterize your top 5.

· **They are handpicked by God, not you, for you.** Your choice is whether you accept them as that or not. You are somehow divinely connected. There is purpose and destiny behind your connection. God knows exactly what he wants, how he wants, where he wants, and when he wants your connection to accomplish his will.

It's amazing how God connects people for his purpose. One summer, I was heading to my hometown to visit my family for the holidays. On the plane ride, I sat next to an extremely friendly lady. I normally don't like to talk on planes but there was something different about this lady. Her greeting was followed by, "do you know Jesus?" She was an evangelist. Realizing she was a believer, we immediately connected and began to talk about some things God had done for us. I ended up giving her a book that I co-authored with a group of women. To say the least, the plane ride home was well spent connecting with her. Little did I know that she knew someone in my Top 5. We saw each other again at this person's birthday party and connected the dots.

- **Area of Expertise.** They are better in some areas than you and can teach you some things. You don't know everything. If you did, then you could fulfill your purpose alone. God doesn't work that way. Even when he created man, he realized Adam couldn't do it all by himself so he created Eve. Our top 5 helps us in our weaknesses and builds upon our strengths.

- **Integrity.** They walk the walk and talk the talk. They do their best to live a holy and righteous lifestyle. They are not perfect but they aim to walk upright and remain in right standing with God daily. They know, love, and live by God's principles.

- **Prayer.** They don't prey on you. They pray for you. They pray God's will and his best for you.

- **Love, Accountability and Authenticity**. They hold you accountable. They're honest in a loving way. Their feedback is constructive and not destructive. They have the right motives. They desire to see God's best for you. They will tell you when you're wrong, hug you through storms, and lift you up when you're down. They help you push through defeat and celebrate with you in victories.

Wise counsel is perhaps one of the most important keys on your journey of faith and focus. There may be times when who you seek counsel from changes. Do so with much prayer and clarity from above.

Prayer: *Heavenly Father, thank you for choosing people for me that you know will help me to walk in the manner worthy of which you called me. Please arrange the individuals in my life in the proper rows, in their proper positions. Please give them wisdom from you that will bless what you called me to do and bless them as well. In Jesus' name. Amen.*

Reflect and Act:

1.Write out your top 5. Pray for about your list. Pray for your list. Do any adjustments or additions need to be made?

2.Besides the criteria listed above, what other criteria do you believe a Top 5 should have?

3.Pray for your Top 5. Ask God to strengthen, heal, and continue to bless them. Pray for your relationships to be covered.

KEY #8 - DISCERNMENT & WISDOM

So give your servant a discerning heart to govern your people and to distinguish between right and wrong. For who can govern this great people of yours?

1 KINGS 3:9

"If any of you lacks wisdom, you should ask God, who gives generously to all without finding fault, and it will be given to you.

JAMES 1:5

Y ears ago there was a popular blind taste test that tested consumers' ability to distinguish between two beverages - Pepsi and Coca-Cola. Someone blindfolded consumers and had them taste both drinks and ask them which they preferred. Afterward, they would take off the blindfold and let them know whether their drink of choice was Pepsi or Coke. It was a test and marketing strategy Pepsi used to see if people truly preferred their drink or the other. Whichever drink you prefer is your choice, but with this witty marketing test speaks volumes to how well we can judge and discern things that may be covered up by a label.

An important part of our faith and focus, discernment is defined as the ability to judge well. In biblical terms, it refers to being able to distinguish a spirit that is truly of God from one that is not. It also refers to being able to distinguish truth from error. In essence, it is good judgment and keen insight.

Discernment can almost come across as knowing about an environment, a person, or a situation through your thoughts, impressions, and other ways that reach your senses. It is not reading someone's mind, but rather knowing whether that person's spirit, heart, and motives are of God or not. Be mindful that even some of the most well-intentioned individuals may have moments when their discernment is a bit off.

Our faith and our focus require that we exercise discernment and seek God about the truth behind an environment, person, or situation. We cannot just stop there. Once we discern a thing, we must take the next step and apply wisdom for how to handle what was discerned. You're aware of a person's intent or motive. How will you handle it if it's not of God? The better question is - **how will you handle it if it is of God**?

God is gracious enough to allow us to come freely and boldly to him to ask for wisdom if we don't know what to do. Wisdom is a compliment to discernment but wisdom is ours for the asking for everyday affairs. He gives it to us freely to help us solve problems, make decisions, and to finish our assignments. Next time, you're not too sure about something, take a minute to stop, drop to your knees, and roll into some prayer to ask the one who knows all things to help you.

Prayer: *Heavenly Father, thank you for the gifts of discernment and wisdom. Please continue to help us* *to properly discern spirits, hearts, seasons, and times. Thank you for continued wisdom for the journey ahead of us and for everyday living.* In Jesus' name. Amen.

Reflect and Act:

1. When have you ever used your discernment in decision making? Was the outcome what you wanted? Do you believe the outcome was what God desired?

2. Things happen in life. Reflect on a time when you could have used some extra wisdom from above. Find one scripture that can apply to that time you needed it. It may be helpful for someone else or in the future.

3. Take some time to dig a bit deeper about the gift of discernment. What did you discover? What applies to where you are on your faith and focus journey?

KEY #9 - CONSISTENCY

*Jesus is the same yesterday,
today and forevermore.*

HEBREWS 13:8

H ave you ever had a routine disrupted? Have you ever been around someone whose routine was interrupted? How did you or they respond? Whether it's a morning, evening, or exercise routine, it makes a difference in your life and at times others.

If you are into wellness or a performer of any sort, you know the importance of consistently practicing to improve. Your practice allows you to make tweaks and improvements over time so that when a "big day" comes you are ready.

Consistency is crucial when it comes to completing an assignment. Knowing what to be consistent with is even more important To maximize our faith and focus, we must be consistent in the things that matter to God. Prayer, praise & worship, fellowship, and reading our Word matters to him.

These are foundational tools in any believer's life. Anyone who is a kingdom builder must exercise these daily. If you work out, you know that results only come through consistent exercise. You cannot expect to look your best if your workout routine is sporadic. You may have the results you want for a while, but soon you will begin to see your body going back to its previous condition.

God appreciates the smallest consistent whispers of praise in a thank you, you're awesome, and you're wonderful.

It is no different in our spiritual lives. Prayer is your lifeline to the Father. It is not an option. 1 Thessalonians 5:16-18 tells us to "always be joyful. Never stop praying. Be thankful in all circumstances, for this is God's will for you who belong to Christ Jesus." Our praise and worship must also be a part of our routine. We shouldn't just lift our hands when we need something or when we finally get the answers to our prayers. Praise God for the little things he does- the activity of your limbs, your security, and the clothes on your back.

Other staples of your spiritual routine include fellowship with others and reading your bible. Make it a priority to get together with others so that you can encourage each other and help to build each other up in the faith. Don't neglect to take time daily to read the bible and discover God's truths about everyday matters. Equally important is asking the Holy Spirit to lead and guide you into the appropriate interpretation and application of the scripture. Far too often, scriptures have been used in a context that God never intended. Ask him to show you what it means and how to apply it. The Word of God is one of the greatest weapons you have. It is key that you will definitely need to utilize daily.

Consider Jesus. Not only was he consistent in prayer, praise, and worship, he was consistent in character. Jesus was consistent in how he dealt with people, his convictions, and his actions. Where there was a need, he met it. Where there was a cry, he heard it. He was the same healer to the woman with the issue of blood, the man at the pool of Bethesda, and the blind beggar. Jesus is the same healer for us today. He is the same, yesterday, today, and forevermore. Let us do our best to follow the consistency Christ modeled.

Prayer: *Heavenly Father, forgive me for past inconsistencies. Help me to build consistency in my prayer life, my praise & worship to you, my fellowship with others, and the time I spend reading the Word. Thank you for helping me to establish and maintain consistency in the areas in my life where they are needed the most. In Jesus' name. Amen.*

Reflect and Act:

1. In which of the areas (prayer, praise & worship, fellowship, or reading the Word) are you most inconsistent? What's one thing that you can do that can help you be more consistent?

2. List 3 things you can incorporate into your daily routine that will help build consistency where you

need it. (i.e. Reading a scripture during a break or devotional time before leaving for work).

3. Find an accountability partner that in strong in an area where you are weak. Ask them to help you in your quest to become consistent. When you're done, reflect on how it has impacted you in that area.

KEY #10 - PROPER PERSPECTIVE

For our present troubles are small and won't last very long. Yet they produce for us a glory that vastly outweighs them and will last forever!

II CORINTHIANS 4:17

I don't know if you have ever checked out Google Maps, Street View, but it is a pretty amazing tool. It allows you to "explore the world at street level". Google and contributors submit photos to the site that allows you to view places around the world through 360-degree street-level imagery. You can explore the Swiss Alps, go beneath the ocean, peek right into the Mount of Olives in Jerusalem, and even visit the Amazon River. You can also see what's right down the street. The best part about it is that it allows you to see 360 degrees around.

A 360-degree perspective is a lot different from life the way we see daily. We cannot always see or understand all that is going on around us, especially amidst some of the chaos, craziness, and confusion that is out there. We don't know what lies ahead of us, but we do know that things happen in life. Matthew 5:45 tells us that it rains on the just and unjust. The good news is that the just live by Faith (Hebrews 10:38). We walk by that firm belief, trusting that God is totally in control of our lives, situations, and circumstances. He will make good on his promises.

There are times in life when we are faced with challenges and changes that can impact our faith and focus. This could be a loss, addition, or an unexpected adjustment. Emotions are naturally a part of the process. When challenged, have you ever stopped, shifted your thinking, and asked God,

"What is the lesson?"

What do I need to get?

What do I need to give up?

These questions allow us to keep things in perspective - which can change over time and shift depending on our position. Consider the following perspectives - bird's eye view, airplane, and panoramic - and how they can influence your faith and focus.

Bird's Eye View

When we look at situations, assignments, or things from this perspective, it is often viewed from a high altitude or distance. Birds can see above things, buildings, trees, and people. They can see things people on land can't see. (They always seem to know when your car is going to be passing by as well. :)

I got a glimpse of a bird's eye view when I was with a friend on a ride at an amusement park. After the screams and laughs, I gained some insight from that ride that I wasn't expecting. I captured it in my journal.

Leah *and I were in line for the Boardwalk Tower, a ride that lifts you up and slowly brings you back down. We were talking about perspective, having mountaintop and valley experiences and how each was important to have. As we went up on the ride, we could see things we couldn't see while we were walking below. We noticed areas we didn't know existed. Perspective. As we were going down we understood that there was an advantage of being able to see the area above. We could see the horizon, some oil rigs, buildings, and movement. After getting off the ride, we had a greater awareness of what was going on around us on the ground because we could see what was going on at the top. Perspective is everything.*

Our ability to scope out the scene was a benefit and blessing to those with us. We were able to navigate the park easier because we knew the layout. Sometimes, reaching a certain level of success, reaching a certain height, or experiencing a particular circumstance can be helpful to others that come behind us. I would dare to say that we have a certain amount of responsibility to help others navigate life's circumstances that we have experienced and overcome.

Airplane

If you have ever flown on an airplane, you are aware that passengers are only able to see out of the sides of the airplane and not in front or behind. Unless you are seated in 1st class, it is tough to see out of the front of a plane. Even then, it is still difficult to see out of the front of the window.

From this perspective, life's situations and circumstances are very similar to a flight. How so? God is the pilot leading and navigating us on our journey. He lifts us and makes sure we land safely from one destination to the next. He sends people into our lives like flight attendants to help us adjust to the flight. They make sure we have what we need to enjoy the flight, stay safe, and teach us how to handle situations should emergencies arise. There are other passengers on the flights that are the people that we encounter throughout life who are headed the same way. We may not always know what is up ahead in detail but we have a general picture of where we are going and what to expect. At times you may get tempted to look back, perhaps look outside the window, but your destiny isn't there. It's in front of you.

It's not necessarily a bad thing that we can't see what is behind us all the time and the details of what's ahead. Sometimes God can't show us what lies ahead because we would mess it up. I know for sure if I knew I would be where I am at in the present moment in my life, I would have definitely asked God for a rain check. "God, can we schedule that for another day? I'll come back." Good thing he didn't.

Panoramic

I love panoramic pictures. It's something about all of these images that aren't supposed to fit into one single image but some how does that makes me smile.

In the past, panoramic paintings and models were a very popular way to represent landscapes and historical events. It started with gluing photos together, but now we have sophisticated technology that allows panoramic to blend beautifully-.Just like these panoramic pictures and the Google Street View, God has full knowledge of what our life will be like – the rises, the falls, and everything in between. He did not make any mistakes when he created you. He knows when we are likely to mess up when we do. He knows the losses we would grieve. He knows the victories we would celebrate. God has the full picture.

While our perspective is limited, His is infinite. He knows exactly what is going on at every moment. With his help, he gives us the ability to shift how we see things. Shifting perspectives is a necessity. To get through life without collecting residue and carrying baggage along with every stop, we need to stop along the way and release the things that can hold us down.

Things are not as coincidental as they seem. Jesus didn't just stumble upon the Samaritan woman at the well. Ruth wasn't just gleaning in the field. You aren't just reading this book by chance. God orchestrates divine moments in our lives. Some of those moments are beautiful, and, other moments are painful. He is with us every step of the way. I don't know about you but I've had beautiful moments and some pretty painful moments. I needed the assurance from God that things were going to be okay and that everything was going to be alright.

At times, it is difficult to wrap your head around some of life's circumstances. To soften life's blows, I try to think of some things as a test. Tests that build our character. Tests that produce the oil needed to fulfill our purpose. Tests that strengthen our faith and give God great glory.

After we get through the tough parts of our faith and focus journey, we have a choice in how we respond. It's with hope that we choose to be like that tree that is planted by the water and refuse to be moved. We can choose to be like the house built on the firm foundation. When the storm came, the house was still standing. Shift how you see things and watch it work out for your good and his glory.

Prayer: *Heavenly Father, thank you for being in charge of my life. You see all things and have all things concerning me under your control. Help me to keep a positive perspective. Help me to shift my perspective when needed even in the midst of storms to see things the way you want me to see them. In Jesus' name. Amen.*

Reflect and Act:

1.Think about a situation you are currently facing. Reflect on how you can shift your thinking in regards to that circumstance. What lesson can you draw from it?

2. To fully understand how perspectives can be shifted, stand on one side of a door. Write or draw what you see. Then go to the other side of the same door and write or draw what you see. What are your thoughts? How can you apply this to your everyday

life?

3.Ask God to align your perspective to his. Observe and record when you begin to see your perception of things change.

KEY #11 - LEARNING
FROM MISTAKES

Fear not; you will no longer live in shame.
Don't be afraid; there is no more disgrace for
you. You will no longer remember the shame of
your youth and the sorrows of widowhood.

ISAIAH 54:4

I'm no stranger to making mistakes. You can probably relate unless you're a part of a few who have never made any mistakes. If you're used to being in control or having things go a certain way, a mistake can be like the end of the world, but they are not. I think mistakes are just those but sometimes they can be God's way of delivering us from a controlling spirit or a spirit of perfection.

But Ashley, who wouldn't want perfection? Perfection is the state of being without a flaw or defect. It may not be a bad thing for some, but is it the right thing? We often confuse perfection with excellence. Excellence means really good, outstanding, or great. Even really great things may have a level of imperfection. There is a perfection that the Bible speaks of that gives us a standard that we should continually aim for. "Be ye perfect, even as your Father which is in heaven is perfect." (Matthew 5:48) Notice the standard for perfection is God, not other people.

Holding a person to a standard God never intended can be harmful. Putting that amount of pressure on someone or yourself to fit into shoes that were only made for God can be crippling spiritually, emotionally, and relationally. We disappoint ourselves when we expect perfection from ourselves and others. People can serve as role models and examples for us but we should never elevate them nor put pressure on them to be who Christ was meant to be for us.

I remember one time I got into it with a

loved one. This person told me, "You're not perfect!" I simply said, "I know," and walked away.
(Everything was resolved later). I sincerely meant
what I said.

There was a time in my life that those words
would have wounded me- a time when I hung on
to the opinion of man and needed validation from
others. Thank God for delivering and healing me of
that! I continue to understand my humanity, that
strives for excellence, but is absolutely no compari-
son for a very BIG and perfect God.

My prayer is that others love me and themselves in spite of imperfections and that we work
on the areas of our lives that do not serve God,
others, or ourselves well. Sometimes we get images
of people in our heads and don't expect them to de-
viate from that image. The only perfect being with a
perfect image is Jesus Christ. Everyday God is allow-
ing us opportunities to perfect our walk and work
towards becoming more like him.

I'm learning that some of the best lessons and
most beautiful things are birthed from mistakes.
I'm always tickled when I think about how a pen-
cil company first profited from people's mistakes.
Thank God for the eraser. After you've made an
error, an eraser allows you to remove it and start

writing all over again. Even with permanent writing tools like a pen, white-out allows for a fresh start. If you're writing with technology, all you have to do is hit the delete button.

I think we all could do a better job of showing grace to ourselves and others from not measuring up from time to time. It takes time and is a process. Gain the lesson from the mistake and aim to make improvements in those areas. There are times when miracles are birthed out of mistakes.

Prayer: *Heavenly Father, thank you for loving us, mistakes and all. Thank you for the grace and mercy you extend to us so that we may extend that same grace and mercy to others. Thank you for the lessons and wisdom that we have gained from mistakes. Please help us not to make costly mistakes and if we have please get the glory. Thank you for making miracles out of mistakes.*

Reflect and Act:

1. Think about a time when you messed up. What is one thing that you learned?

2. Think about a time someone made a mistake with you. How did the situation turn out? Find a

scripture that can help you deal with the situation.

3. In what area can you grow and work on having a spirit of excellence?

KEY #12 - PERSEVERANCE

Because of our faith, Christ has brought us into this place of underserved privilege where we now stand, and we confidently and joyfully look forward to sharing God's glory. We can rejoice when we run into problems and trials, for we know that they help us develop endurance. And endurance develops strength of character, and character strengthens our confident hope of salvation. And this hope will not lead to disappointment. For we know how God loves us, because he has given us the Holy Spirit to fill our hearts with his love.

ROMANS 5:2-5

Have you ever had a time in your life when you felt like you were in the boxing ring? It may have felt as i you were fighting with all your might only to get the wind knocked out of you. You muster up some strength but then here comes another unexpected blow. It's not a fun or easy place. There was a season in my life where hit after hit left me discouraged and wanting to throw in the towel. I was exhausted, losing hope, wondering what was the point. It was a very bad place and I was in bad shape. To make matters worse, it seemed as if everything happened at once. I felt like quitting everything and everyone - but then I got a second wind.

Just like a runner gets a second wind, the Holy Spirit breathed life into me. God breathed life into me through the prayers of the righteous and my loved ones. He breathed on me during worship. He breathed the breath of life into me during the time spent in his presence studying the Word. He breathed life into me when he led me to recall words His words spoken over my life, look, visions given to me on vision boards, and in business plans. He breathed life into me when people called or messaged out of the blue just to say hello. He breathed life into me when his promises of restoration manifested. Friends, if you are going to last and walk this faith and focus journey for the long haul, it is going to take perseverance.

Perseverance, tenacity, stamina, grit- different versions of the same characteristic. You need it. We're told to fight the good fight of faith. I'll be honest. There will be times when you get tired of fighting. It's in those moments when you get vulnerable with God and let him know it's too much. It is in our weaknesses that his strength is perfected. You don't have to fight alone. What's even better is that some battles are not even yours. God will handle them. We just have to step aside and let him. It's not always easy but it's also not always hard. God is gracious, loving, and kind. He knows when it's time to raise a standard, give you some more grace, and replenish you so that you can finish your faith and focus journey.

Prayer: *Heavenly Father, thank you for giving me strength for this journey. Thank you for strength and victory over every battle. Forgive me when I've tried to do things on my own. Please fill me up when I'm empty, refresh me when I'm dry, be my strength when I'm weak and be my sight when I cannot see. Help me to persevere and overcome. In Jesus' name. Amen.*

Reflect and Act:

1. What scriptures have helped you when you have wanted to give up?

2. What encourages you when you feel like throwing in the towel or need a boost?

3. Perseverance looks different for everyone. Reflect on a time you came through a difficult time. What helped you then that can help you or others now?

REACHING FOR THE PRIZE

No, dear brothers and sisters, I have not
achieved it, but I focus on this one thing:
Forgetting the past and looking forward to
what lies ahead, I press on to reach the end
of the race and receive the heavenly prize for
which God, through, Christ Jesus, is calling us.

PHILIPPIANS 3:13 - 14

Y ou now have twelve keys to put into your toolkit for your faith and focus journey. Peter used them to walk on the water. Jesus used them to complete his assignment to reconcile humanity back to God. You can use them on your journey to walk out your purposes. These aren't the only ones you have access to, but they are a good start.

Prayer: *Heavenly Father, thank you for your unconditional love. May every key be used in a way that pleases you. May I continue to seek your face, hear you clearly, and enjoy your presence. May I walk in faith, in humility, filtering out every lie of the enemy. May I have good counsel that is handpicked by you, walk with discernment, wisdom, and consistency. Thank you for the proper perspective and wisdom gained from mistakes made whether they were mine or someone else's. May I continue to operate in the grace that you give us daily and persevere through it all. I praise you for your love. Thank you for providing the things that I need to continue on my faith and focus journey. In Jesus' name. Amen.*

STUDYING THE SCRIPTURE

I t would be a disservice to leave out one of the most fundamental keys you need in your arsenal as a believer. Scriptures outlined in God's word are critical to maintaining your faith and focus. His word, correctly understood and applied, is powerful. In the pages to come are scriptures centered on faith and focus. I encourage you to study them, dissect them, ask God for clarity and understanding, and apply them to your life. It always helps to have a way to study scripture. If you don't have a go to method, here is one that you can use. I hope it helps you dig deep to stay the course.

OIA (Observe - Interpret - Analyze)
Scripture Study Method

This method is ideal using one line of scripture. It is essentially a way you can break down the scriptures to better understand what it means and how to apply it to your life to see manifested change. Please keep in mind that as you study, it is in your best interest to ask the Holy Spirit for guidance, correct interpretation, and appropriate application. *Trust in the Lord with all your heart, lean not unto your own understanding, in all your ways acknowledge him and he will direct your path.* (Proverbs 3:5-6) He will direct your path as you study.

As with any study, it starts with a ready mind, willing heart and a conducive learning environment. Grab your favorite writing tools, notebook or journal, and a bible. Now you're ready to go.

Step One

The first step in the OIA scripture study method is to observe. Look at every single word in the scripture. What do you see? What words stick out at you? Distinguish those from others by highlighting, circling, or underlining them. Let's use this

Matthew 14:27 as an example.

But <u>Jesus</u> spoke to them <u>at once.</u> "Don't be <u>afraid</u>," he said. "<u>Take courage</u>. I am <u>here</u>!"

Next, find out what these words mean. It's as simple as using a dictionary. To get the full effect of what God intended for you to understand, use a biblical dictionary and always consult the Holy Spirit asking him to help you land on the appropriate definition.

But <u>Jesus</u> spoke to them <u>at once.</u> "Don't be <u>afraid</u>," he said. "<u>Take courage</u>. I am <u>here</u>!"

Jesus

- Free Dictionary (Online Dictionary) - A teacher and prophet born in Bethlehem and active in Nazareth; his life and sermons form the basis for Christianity
- Bible Dictionary- Christ is the official name of our Lord; to distinguish him from other so called, he is spoken of as "Jesus of Nazareth" (John 18:70, and "Jesus son of Joseph" (John 6:42), and much more

At once

- Free Dictionary (Online Dictionary) - Immediately
- Bible Dictionary- Without the intervention of any other case of event; opposed to mediately; instantly, at the present time; without delay, or the intervention of time

Afraid

- Free Dictionary (Online Dictionary) Feeling fear
- Bible Dictionary - Impressed with fear or apprehension; fearful, This word expresses a less degree of fear than terrified or frightened. It is followed by of before the object of fear; as, to be afraid of death

Take

- Free Dictionary (Online Dictionary) - To get into one's hands, control, or possession of
- Bible Dictionary - no different definition found

Courage

- Free Dictionary (Online Dictionary) - A quality of spirit that enables you to face danger or pain without showing fear

- Bible Dictionary - Bravery; intrepidity, that quality or mind which enables men to encounter danger and difficulties with firmness, or without fear or depression of spirits, valor, boldness, resolution. Be strong and of good courage (Deuteronomy 31)

Here

- Free Dictionary (Online Dictionary) - At or in this place, at this time, now, in the present life or condition,
- Bible Dictionary - no different definition found

Step Two

The second step in the OIA scripture study method is to interpret the scripture. What do the words mean? **How can you make sense of the words that stood out to you?** What revelation did you get? Write down any ahas that you get.

> But Jesus spoke to them at once. "Don't be afraid," he said. "Take courage. I am here!"

Ahas

- ·This scripture was in reference to the disciples being out to sea on a boat in the middle of a storm so the disciples are terrified. They are scared because of the storm raging around them and because they see a man walking towards them who appears to be a ghost.

- They screamed and Jesus (the son of God, God in the flesh) spoke to them immediately. He came to their rescue right away. He didn't wait.

- He told them don't be scared. Release the fear you have and take hold of courage. Be brave because he was there with them. Now far off, but right there physically present by the boat walking on the water that was just early raging around them.

Step Three

The final step of the OIA scripture study method is to apply the scripture to your own life. We have Scripture as a guide. **What do these words mean in light of your OWN life? How can you make sense of them? What can you apply to your life for**

you to experience victory in an area? If you would like to take it one step further, you can turn your revelations, insights, and applications into a prayer. Stay hopeful. Stay expectant.

> **But Jesus spoke to them at once. "Don't be afraid," he said. "Take courage. I am here!"**

Application
- If I experience a storm or something scary in my life, God will be right there to help me. The Holy Spirit is my everyday comforter in times of trouble, ensuring me that it will be okay.

SCRIPTURES ON FAITH [NLT]

Hebrews 11:1 - Faith shows the reality of what we hope for; it is the evidence of things we cannot see.

Hebrews 11:6 - And it is impossible to please God without faith. Anyone who wants to come to him must believe that God exists and that he rewards those who sincerely seek him.

Matthew 21:21 - 22 - Then Jesus told them, "I tell you the truth, if you have faith and don't doubt, you can do things like this and much more. You can even say to this mountain, 'May you be lifted up and thrown into the sea,' and it will happen. You can pray for anything, and if you have faith, you will receive it."

Romans 1:17 - This Good News tells us how God makes us right in his sight. This is accomplished from start to finish by faith. As the Scriptures say, "It is through faith that a righteous person has life."

Romans 10:17 - So faith comes from hearing, that is, hearing the Good News about Christ.

1 Corinthians 2:5 - I did this so you would trust not in human wisdom but in the power of God.

Luke 1:37 - For the word of God will never fail.

2 Corinthians 5:7 - For we live by believing and not by seeing.

James 1:5 -6 - If you need wisdom, ask our generous God, and he will give it to you. He will not rebuke you for asking. But when you ask him, be sure that your faith is in God alone. Do not waver, for a person with divided loyalty is as unsettled as a wave of the sea that is blown and tossed by the wind.

Mark 9:23 - "What do you mean, 'If I can'?" Jesus asked. "Anything is possible if a person believes."

Mark 11:24 - I tell you, you can pray for anything, and if you believe that you've received it, it will be yours.

John 11:25-26 - Jesus told her, "I am the resurrection and the life. Anyone who believes in me will live, even after dying. Everyone who lives in me and believes in me will never ever die. Do you believe this, Martha?"

Mark 10:52 - And Jesus said to him, "Go, for your faith has healed you." Instantly the man could see, and he followed Jesus down the road.

Hebrews 11:11 - It was by faith that even Sarah was able to have a child, though she was barren and was too old. She believed that God would keep his promise.

John 3:16 - "For this is how God loved the world: He gave his one and only Son, so that everyone who believes in him will not perish but have eternal life.

1 Corinthians 16:13 - 14 Be on guard. Stand firm in

the faith. Be courageous. Be strong. And do everything with love.

Acts 16:31 - They replied, "Believe in the Lord Jesus and you will be saved, along with everyone in your household."

James 2:17 - So you see, faith by itself isn't enough. Unless it produces good deeds, it is dead and useless.

Matthew 17:20 - "You don't have enough faith," Jesus told them. "I tell you the truth, if you had faith even as small as a mustard seed, you could say to this mountain, 'Move from here to there,' and it would move. Nothing would be impossible."

John 7:38 - Anyone who believes in me may come and drink! For the Scriptures declare, 'Rivers of living water will flow from his heart."

Romans 5:1 - Therefore, since we have been made right in God's sight by faith, we have peace with God because of what Jesus Christ our Lord has done for us.

John 20:29 - Then Jesus told him, "You believe because you have seen me. Blessed are those who believe without seeing me."

John 11:40 - Jesus responded, "Didn't I tell you that you would see God's glory if you believe?"

1 Peter 1:8-9 - You love him even though you have never seen him. Though you do not see him now, you trust him; and you rejoice with a glorious, inexpressible joy. The reward for trusting him will be the salvation of your souls.

James 1:3 - For you know that when your faith is tested, your endurance has a chance to grow.

1 Timothy 6:11 - But you, Timothy, are a man of God; so run from all these evil things. Pursue righteousness and a godly life, along with faith, love, perseverance, and gentleness.

Matthew 21:22 - You can pray for anything, and if you have faith, you will receive it."

Colossians 3:12 - Since God chose you to be the holy people he loves, you must clothe yourselves with tenderhearted mercy, kindness, humility, gentleness, and patience.

Psalm 25:9 - He leads the humble in doing right, teaching them his way.

Micah 6:8 - Do justly, love mercy and walk humbly with your God.

Genesis 15:6 And Abram believed the Lord, and the Lord counted him as righteous because of his faith.

SCRIPTURES ON FOCUS [NLT]

Philippians 3:12- 16 - I don't mean to say that I have already achieved these things or that I have already reached perfection. But I press on to possess that perfection for which Christ Jesus first possessed me. No, dear brothers and sisters, I have not achieved it, but I focus on this one thing: Forgetting the past and looking forward to what lies ahead, I press on to reach the end of the race and receive the heavenly prize for which God, through Christ Jesus, is calling us. Let all who are spiritually mature agree on these things. If you disagree on some point, I believe God will make it plain to you. But we must hold on to the progress we have already made.

Hebrews 12:2 - We do this by keeping our eyes on Jesus, the champion who initiates and perfects our faith. Because of the joy awaiting him, he endured the cross, disregarding its shame. Now he is seated in the place of honor beside God's throne.

Proverbs 4:25 - Look straight ahead, and fix your eyes on what lies before you.

Proverbs 4:27 - Don't get sidetracked; keep your feet from following evil.

Colossians 3:2 - Think about the things of heaven, not the things of earth.

Philippians 4:6 - Don't worry about anything; instead, pray about everything. Tell God what you need, and thank him for all he has done.

Isaiah 26:3 - You will keep in perfect peace all who trust in you, all whose thoughts are fixed on you!

Isaiah 41:10 - Don't be afraid, for I am with you. Don't be discouraged, for I am your God. I will strengthen you and help you. I will hold you up with my victorious right hand.

Isaiah 43:18 - But forget all that—it is nothing compared to what I am going to do.

Psalm 1:1-6 Oh, the joys of those who do not follow the advice of the wicked, or stand around with sinners, or join in with mockers. But they delight in the law of the Lord, meditating on it day and night. They are like trees planted along the riverbank, bearing fruit each season.
Their leaves never wither, and they prosper in all they do.
But not the wicked! They are like worthless chaff, scattered by the wind.They will be condemned at the time of judgment. Sinners will have no place among the godly.
For the Lord watches over the path of the godly, but the path of the wicked leads to destruction.

Psalm 16:8 - I know the Lord is always with me. I will not be shaken, for he is right beside me.

Psalm 25:15 - My eyes are always on the Lord, for he rescues me from the traps of my enemies.

Psalm 86:11 -Teach me your ways, O Lord, that I

may live according to your truth! Grant me purity of heart, so that I may honor you.

Psalm 141:8 - I look to you for help, O Sovereign Lord. You are my refuge; don't let them kill me.

Psalm 119:15 - I will study your commandments and reflect on your ways.

Proverbs 2:2-5 - Tune your ears to wisdom, and concentrate on understanding. Cry out for insight, and ask for understanding. Search for them as you would for silver; seek them like hidden treasures. Then you will understand what it means to fear the Lord, and you will gain knowledge of God.

Matthew 6:33 - Seek the Kingdom of God above all else, and live righteously, and he will give you everything you need.

Matthew 24:42 - So you, too, must keep watch! For you don't know what day your Lord is coming.

Philippians 2:2 - Then make me truly happy by agreeing wholeheartedly with each other, loving one another, and working together with one mind and purpose.

Philippians 4:8 - And now, dear brothers and sisters, one final thing. Fix your thoughts on what is true, and honorable, and right, and pure, and lovely, and admirable. Think about things that are excellent and worthy of praise

2 Timothy 2:15 - Work hard so you can present yourself to God and receive his approval. Be a good worker, one who does not need to be ashamed and who correctly explains the word of truth.

Romans 12:2 - Don't copy the behavior and customs of this world, but let God transform you into a new person by changing the way you think. Then you will learn to know God's will for you, which is good and pleasing and perfect.

Psalm 32:8 - The Lord says, "I will guide you along the best pathway for your life. I will advise you and watch over you.

Colossians 3:1-4 - Since you have been raised to new life with Christ, set your sights on the realities of heaven, where Christ sits in the place of honor at God's right hand. **2** Think about the things of heaven, not the things of earth. **3** For you died to this life, and your real life is hidden with Christ in God. **4** And when Christ, who is your[a] life, is revealed to the whole world, you will share in all his glory.

Proverbs 3:5-6 - Trust in the Lord with all your heart; do not depend on your own understanding. Seek his will in all you do, and he will show you which path to take.

1 Peter 1:13 - So prepare your minds for action and exercise self-control. Put all your hope in the gracious salvation that will come to you when Jesus Christ is revealed to the world.

Acts 20:24 - But my life is worth nothing to me unless I use it for finishing the work assigned me by the Lord Jesus—the work of telling others the Good News about the wonderful grace of God.

Proverbs 16:3 - Commit your actions to the Lord, and your plans will succeed.

Philippians 4:13 For I can do everything through Christ, who gives me strength.

ACKNOWLEDGEMENTS

Thank you God for your unfailing, extravagant love and its benefits. Thank you to the family, friends, co-laborers, and strangers who contributed in any way to the production of this book. This journey started years ago when I first realized that focus this was one of the many keys needed to complete any major task and to live as a victorious believer. May you benefit from the seeds you've sown into my purpose and His plans.

ABOUT THE AUTHOR

Ashley M. Martin

"You learn something new every-thing" is a philosophy Ashley M. Martin lives by. She successfully blends her love for educating, en-couraging, and empowering other into dynamic conversations, coaching sessions and talks.

After ten years serving in the public school system, she took a leap of faith and followed her heart expanding her work as an author and speaker. Not All Fs Are Bad is one of the works she has written. She serves the next generation through a social enterprise that equips them to become leaders and entrepreneurs.

Ashley holds a B.A. in Psychology from Scripps College (Claremont, CA) and a Masters of Educational Leadership from the University of St. Thomas (Houston, TX). Ashley lives by Matthew 6:33 and loves journals, tea, most things gold,creating, and travel.

Website: www.iamashleym.com
Email: info@iamshleym.com
Social Media: @ashleym3710

REFERENCES

Donne, John. Meditation XVII: No Man is An Island. 1624. http://isu.indstate.edu/ilnprof/ENG451/IS-LAND/.February 22, 2020.

"Revelation." (2020). The Free Dictionary. Retrieved from https://www.thefreedictionary.com/revelation on May 20,2020.

"Realization." (2020). The Free Dictionary. Retrieved from https://www.thefreedictionary.com/realization on May 20,2020.

"Jesus." (2020). The Free Dictionary. Retrieved from https://www.thefreedictionary.com/jesus on May 20,2020.

"At once" (2020). The Free Dictionary. Retrieved from https://www.thefreedictionary.com/atonce on May 20,2020.

"Afraid" (2020). The Free Dictionary. Retrieved from https://www.thefreedictionary.com/afraid on May 20,2020.

"Take" (2020). The Free Dictionary. Retrieved from https://www.thefreedictionary.com/take on May 20,2020.

"Courage." (2020). The Free Dictionary. Retrieved from https://www.thefreedictionary.com/courage on May 20,2020.

"Here." (2020). The Free Dictionary. Retrieved from https://www.thefreedictionary.com/here on May 20,2020.

All bible dictionary definitions retrieved from https://www.biblestudytools.com/dictionaries/.